A SUITCASEFUL OF DOG

Sue Vickerman has published five poetry books and four works of fiction and edits for Naked Eye Publishing. Her poems and articles have appeared in *Stand*, *The Rialto*, *The North*, *The Guardian*, and *The Times Educational Supplement*, and her story and poem translations in *The Poetry Review*, *Oxford Poetry*, *Modern Poetry in Translation*, *The Shanghai Review*, and *The Los Angeles Review*. Her two full length translations from German are a volume of Kathrin Schmidt's poems and Schmidt's short story collection. She is a northerner and lives in Yorkshire.

Also by Sue Vickerman

Shag   (Arrowhead Press, 2003;
                                                Naked Eye Publishing, 2017)

The social decline of the oystercatcher   (Biscuit Publishing Ltd, 2005;
                                                Naked Eye Publishing, 2022)

Kunst by 'Suki'   (Indigo Dreams Publishing, 2012)

Thin bones like wishbones   (Indigo Dreams Publishing 2013)

Adventus   (Naked Eye Publishing 2017)

CONTENTS

ISBN: 978-1-917617-13-0

Cover designed by Aaron Kent

Cover image: © Varbenov / Adobe Stock

Edited and Typeset by Aaron Kent

Broken Sleep Books Ltd
PO BOX 102
Llandysul
SA44 9BG

To Mike

a suitcaseful of dog

Sue Vickerman

Broken Sleep Books

MY TREE SWING

After the storm our sycamore's
left limb is still double-shackled as before
with offcuts of zinc-plated chain
nicked by my Opa from the steelworks
he jobbed at after they got here

but the tree is now uprooted
(Oma's and Opa's fate) and slung
across the torrent that yesterday
was a pavement, like an arm to escape on.
Gone, my childhood swing from way back when.

Fact is, the tree was never destined to last,
fated by a fungus attack two decades ago.
How Oma cried on finding it to be hollow,
like a dream gone. Now the whole thing's gone,
tackled down, drowned, gone to where they've gone.

I spot something black, the seat of my swing,
inhumanly swollen, and more storms to come.

AFTER THE BLAST

the shadow of his wingspan still tickling the blood-soaked frock
of a little girl like carrion among others bleeding on the playground
between St Michael's Church and the village shop—
how could we have been so distracted, you taking snaps,
me witnessing him through my field-glasses, short-necked
wings dark-tipped in a shallow V, his call like a cat's

gliding, now, above the shattered children
when we dash over, their breaths quick and shallow—
a hole in a shoulder, an eye gone, dustbin men
running, bird-song, normal school-bell, a child's wail...
Those red berries bubbling from mouths
are in his sights, see his finely-barred fanned tail

our commonest most widespread bird of prey,
but they're taking over, they're taking over the country –

IN ALL HER YEARS AT THE BAKERY

where they'd rise under her motherly eye—
baps and bloomers, oven-bottom buns,
wheat, spelt, rye and that French line
shining bronzed like knotted muscle –
where, at taking-out time, she'd insert
the great flat oven-peel under those rows of
hot fat bums, listening to Radio 2
while the young ones flirted

no-one knows why, not her co-workers
who come running when they smell skin
welding to the oven and find her broad bottom
bending in, all the years, why she's leaned in,
why risk bread bouncing with abandon
all over the tiles, what compulsion after
all the happy years and two grandchildren,
this reaching in, this longing, this attack
on common sense, against all regs
she's reached right to the back
of the red-hot rack and
ripped from the brioche a *bouchon*.

DEAD DOG

My friend's dead dog in a suitcase,
a dog-sitting favour gone wrong,
my friend in Torremolinos, oblivious,
dead dog on the underground
on the way to my mum's back garden,
train jam-packed

and I'm almost certain the
bearded man I'm pressed against
is the Archbishop of Canterbury,
and it feels meant to be,
an expert sent to me, this bearded man
on a jam-packed train
on the way to my mum's back garden,
friend in Torremolinos oblivious,
dog-sitting favour gone wrong,
how friendships can be lifelong or end in
bust-ups while life just pisses on regardless,
suitcaseful of dog in rigor mortis.

I WANT YOU TO KNOW

how I've been since you left. I want you to know
that I think about you. I want you to know
what a girl said to me on the bus on the way
to the job I've picked up since you left: you look
like KD Lang, she said. Just what *you* said!
Do you know how many onions I've grown?
I want you to know not that I want you but
how my culinary skills have improved.
Me! Cooking! Beans a-la-toast avec champignons.
You're all over the world now but I just want you I
want you to know I still want to know you.

MENOPAUSING BESIDE THE DUCKPOND

gree-ee-ee-ee-ee-een stiletto-slim pins,
slinky reeds stick-thin as a heron's legs,
like knife-blades they waver from slits
in the water, dangerously lovely

but the pond is foul: brackish, thick-
surfaced, edges clogged with black crud
like stopped blood, with duck-shit, with a duck
long past laying eggs—fat but dead,

and me, puffy-ankled and stinking,
my bra soaked, while those minxes poke
at the sky, tall as they can, pricking at
anything scudding by till something pops.

I ALWAYS SAID THE CHANGES WERE PORTENTS.

Changing climate. How our Christmases
changed. Remember the long run of Advents
we spent on a cliff-edge? Snowflakes
cartwheeling off it then downwards,
down over ledges clogged with seabirds—
how they clung on—the beyond unknown

and how we clung on—the beyond unknown,
and our strung-up simple cardboard stars,
and wrapping up, unwrapping, thanking.
Later we'd pull crackers, joke, snack on
left-overs, read our stocking books, televise.
But cardboard was so wrong, and the story
we'd believed in all along

for the hills had begun to burn, carbon
curtaining everything. And storm after storm.
One raged in from the sea and took our home.
No meaning. And people saw the change in us.
Remember our rows in coffee shops—milk
hissing out of little chrome pipes, us hissing?
Till breath-stopping gales stopped even those.

Peace and goodwill came again. In a cottage
in Wales. Welsh dresser, pear tree in a pot
in the yard. But it was pointless—one sole pear,
that bloody church bell, the age-speckled mirror
reflecting bodies no longer limpeted onto each other.
And so to farewells. Goodbye to the button-back
chair, to the smells—mulled wine, candles—

to each other. Does reading this
make you miss me, make you regret
abandoning the love that came down?
Such loss. Though random words linger—
French hens, calling birds, cradle. Alone
on the twenty-fifth I scrub at your cup stains,
five gold rings you merrily left on the table.

A MESSAGE AFTER THE BEEP

Bev! Listen—I've got summat to say.
By the way, I'm done here and
it's been worse than sad. Horrendous.
Chapel packed, but crap. No proper plan,
no format. Not even a whip-round for that
place he detoxed in, or Free Palestine,
summat important to Martin.
No songs, no vicar, but why no humanist?
Just his brother, pissed. Pathetic.

Then we're outside, course it's raining isn't it
and I put up the brolly I bought changing trains
at Birmingham but it's flaming broken—
you feel bloody silly if a spoke's gone when
you've a smart suit on—and we're knee-deep in
mud and staring at a coffin wi' nowt on it coz
the brother's card said no flowers, it actually said
Merry Christmas, the funeral was a Post-It Note.

Then Adrian who found him

the lad who actually found him

why did it take nine days?

But he can't talk for crying

so nothing important gets said about
who Martin was; that he was...

And worse: the pub! Shut! No wake!
They hadn't even ordered in a plate of
open bloody sandwiches godsake so everybody
sets off through the streets
seeking another hostelry, but rain's
coming down in sheets and I'm soaked
and no-one speaks to me and then thank christ
a taxi comes along so I'm back at the Jury's Inn.

No way was that the send-off he deserved.
It's been shocking. Grim is the word.
Because no-one really knew him
although it was packed, folk asking why? Why?
No-one should leave this planet wi' nowt said.
No proper eulogy, no facts. No-one
stood up, nobody just stood up and...
Bev, shall we get wed?

Helluva day, suit jacket sopping,
this god-awful room's got no heater in it,
he should've had a Guardian obit,
he was a hundred percent. So how about it?
How come he had a gun, anyway?
Let's move. Let's buy a camper van and
move somewhere, Orkney, an island,
somewhere tight-knit, have kids

coz everything he didn't have was why.

And this tie's ruined.

THE SWEET CUPBOARD

Think of a doll's house.
Hardboard walls quartering it.
Little doors between each quarter.
Hinged wooden people
propped in armchairs
or straightened out on beds.

Things they might yell through the walls
about supper, schoolwork, mucky boots,
hogging the bathroom they're not allowed to lock.

Out-of-scale furniture fills the space.
This kitchen table that does for
mending bikes on, putting a vase on,
the man to read his newspaper on.
See the beds, how they're crammed in,
how narrow, how hard it must be to breathe.

Four small rooms—four boxes up-on-end,
no more than an eighth of an inch between each.
Open the little hinged cupboard; find, in among,
the empty sweet tin, and pretend.

THE PISSAN FAMILY

Kaizen is a Japanese business philosophy of fostering team spiritedness among workers and encouraging them to seek out and remove inefficiencies, thereby constantly improving productivity.

It was knocking off time when they put the news out. Like a punch. Kaizen was down in Keith's locker between Keith's Pissan sponge-bag and Pissan coffee mug, buried under a towel (Pissan) still wet from Keith's shower after a squash game post-lunch.

That's Kaizen our works mascot, "won" by the chief exec's PA (ask not) in the Secret Santa in the plant's first year. For a decade it sat floppy-eared on the flat top of the PA's PC till the supervisors took it over. Taking turns. It's Keith's today. Kaizen's fur, by the way, is a bit greyer these days—aren't we all.

But the plant's spotless. Always was. And vast: we're the size of a city. As in, fifty football pitches and one almighty conveyor-belt that's on all the time. Time being the operative word: time is crucial. Nothing must stop the production line's rotation. Rotation being the operative word: our shifts roll on. We are a relay team, team being the operative word too

till this week's drip-feed of bad news coming over the tannoy: declining car sales, the industry's new low; prohibitive set-up costs re: the X-Trak, and now, today's shock. Final blow. It's not that they're pulling a vehicle, they say, but it's 'no' to the new model. They're moving its base after all. To Europe.

Bugger 'lucky mascot'! Although not a Pissan dog, Kaizen takes the flack. All mine and Sue's plans, all these years of hard graft, all the pats on the back. Sue, who triggered a kaizen blitz by spotting a shortcut for the bots that transport small parts round the plant. Team my arse. How could my Sue be awarded *zenkai* status, and now this

this Pissan farce, this change of mind, seven thousand dependents on Teeside still reeling from the loss of the mines, the forty thousand UK-wide. Women. Children. The Pissan family. To those cyberminds, we're logistics. Just cogs in their machines. Capitalism!—spits Paul, our union man on his soap box in the club later.

Me and Sue—we met and married here. Never mind that planned week in Malta to celebrate our imminent twenty-fifth, or our dream of a timeshare. Forget Macarthy and Stone for the mum-in-law. Think shuttered shops. Shut pubs. Men have died for less than this. 'Pissan family'—taking the piss, says Paul, pissed, six pints in.

That mucky mut got chucked in the Tyne by Keith, arseholed, walking back to the house he was born in. *This puts the lid on me putting my old mum in a serviced bungalow and doing some dating again.* He was gutted. Obviously that was the mascot he chucked in the river. Keith is not a cruel man.

Footnote: we weren't even worth a branded Pissan dog. It was a Snoopy.

ARE YOU ASLEEP

while i'm still up
ironing your shirts
or are you sneaking looks
at my rush-job
just fronts collar and cuffs

my arm's aching

it's late

would you sense
if the tip of my iron
nicked the skin of this pink
poplin slim-fit ted baker
would you hear the rip
smell the scorch feel the burn
whimper?

VIGIL

Open the window to birdsong to help keep her alive.
That big fat blackbird *ha ha*! will keep her alive, and
how lovely the wildflower meadow was near Askrigg
that time, and pushing Janet on the swings,
chapel Gang Shows. Keeping her mouth moist will
keep her alive, and singing along to *The Hills are Alive*
will keep her alive, and playing the whole of *Oklahoma*.
Keep stroking her arm (and keep back the sad news
about Donald). Dad's downstairs looking at photos!

This year's May-blossom's pretty. Like froth!
You can't see it from here. Are you awake, here's
your straw, the sun's gone in, are you alright, are you
warm enough, Bev's had rain for their wedding,
such a pity, I'll just tuck you in, I'm just off to the toilet,
I'll just pull this up a bit, I think I'd better ask them to
change it, I'll just go get a cup of tea, I'll
go see if, I'll pull the curtains on for you, I'll
stop over tonight so I'll just be through the wall.

I'll go see if Dad's alright now, d'you want
Dad? I'll send him up, I'll be back.

OUT WALKING LAST NIGHT IN WINTRY WEATHER

I froze. Stopped short. The hail stopped
arrowing down, stopping mid-air, some stones of it
suspended above the asphalt after bouncing.

Frozen was not the word for her bloodied head
or naked fingers, they were still hot but
she was dead. I felt a chill in my bones.

Then the hail began pounding again, as it should,
as I phoned and waited, her hands now
blueing and whitening chameleon-like,
hail settling into her wrinkled skin and
the folds of her nighty, confirming her deadness,
and onto the asphalt—thick enough to shovel.

PEN POISED FOR THE DAY'S FIRST BLACK LOOP

The bedroom of the lighthouse
full of double bed and dull north light.
A wooden-shuttered window. Desk.
Desk lamp. Hung on the door hooks,
coats—a bulk as big as a big man.
Beneath the bed, boxes. Of shoes.
Of books. The bed is all. Desk small,
wedged right up to this curved window,
daylight bathing the room in dullness.

I stare out. Sea. The slow strobe of a light
in the dull light, how it strokes the grey
with a beam of white. Grey filling my page.
A coffee ring has rusted it. Beyond is world;
in here just morning, looming, and beyond
the radio noise, the huge sea shushing

till out of the white, the shush, the grey, the sea, the light
leaps a black loop! *First porpoise of the day,* I write.

GO MOVE MAT

To do, before I wake up dead
on the bathmat: have a clear-out,
voice-record my memoirs of Bradford,
try Aiyla's recipe for flatbread,
finish writing my poetry book
entitled *Old? Fuck that*.
The grandchildren, great
grandchildren, need to be told
what it was like way back.
No internet. Wait till Starwars
brings down the satellites,
you'll know then

it was better. Before recycling,
before the solar panel on the shed,
when no-one knocked first and
white sliced bread was good and dogs
ran free. At ninety-three I haven't said
all that needs to be said
and I can't hear what's said back,
but I know re-using plastic bags
won't cut it. Elect Aiyla—get this lot
out. By force, even. Go tree-planting.
Next-doors have taken a refugee.
My lawn is now potatoes. Of course
tonight, when I get out of bed for a pee
I might trip on the mat and hit my head
(mental note: go move mat) but more likely

I'll make tea and jot poems into the wee hours.
Climate. Covid. Brexit. Alastair isolating
in America. Good apple year.

MIRANDA'S DINNER-PLATE INSTALLATION

SCENARIO: *Student common room, the morning after the Art Foundation Course party. Everyone stoned and happy*

OFF STAGE: SMASH!

GIRL (O.S.): That's what I think of your hand-painted dicks lifted straight from Judy Chicago, you copy-cat man-stealing [SPOTLIGHT ON GIRL FISTING CHOCOLATE-CHIP COOKIE DOUGH INTO MOUTH] anorexic witch [SMASH] leaving your junk [SMASH] food on the side to make me fat [SMASH]—wish this was your face—and this one's [SMASH] for shagging Shit-head Pat when he'd just crawled out of *my* bed to go for a slash [SMASH]—that's for you, Patrick! Fuckwit.

SPOTLIGHT OFF

A SHARD SHOOTS INTO COMMON ROOM UNDER CONNECTING DOOR. THEY TURN UP AMY WINEHOUSE TO DROWN OUT MORE PLATES CRASHING ONTO ARTROOM FLOOR, AS AMY CROONS—WHEN WILL WE GET THE TIMES TO BE JUST FRIENDS?—AS PENULTIMATE PLATE SNAPS CLEAN IN HALF OVER TAP AND GAGGING NOISE IS HEARD

SPOTLIGHT ON

GIRL PUSHING TWO FINGERS DOWN
THROAT TILL ALL THAT IS IN HER SPRAYS
OVER THE DRAINER. SHE SMASHES THE
FINAL PLATE OVER AN EASEL, LAUGHING
SO HARD THAT AT LAST PATRICK COMES
IN, SENT AS CLASS REP TO DEAL WITH
WHO IS FREAKING

GIRL: Hi Pat! [OFFERS ROLL-UP WHILE PULLING
             HER CARDIGAN OVER THE SICK ON HER
             TOP] —got a little bit of weed in it—[SMILES
             SUNNILY]—we still speaking? Your collage-y
             pastiche thing about trans with bits done in
             lipstick is really, really interesting.

BLACKOUT

MUCH LATER [LIGHTS UP] PATRICK SLIPS
BACK INTO COMMON ROOM

GENERAL MERRIMENT AT HIS APPEARANCE

STUDENT: Been working on your final project then Patrick,
             ho ho—

PAT: [SHELL-SHOCKED] Fuck off —I've just
             accidentally got engaged. Where's Miranda? She's
             going to go bal-list-ic.

LIGHTS OUT

SAVING THE WHIRLED

Select a 'doing' word,
a present simple one.
Translate it into another tongue
then another until you
have a collection. Five.
List all five verbs. Now
look and listen as side by side
they work/think/go bowling/
have a drink/date/leap in the pool/
fret about the planet/mate –

listen to how young ones that
beggar definition are born,
and are borne on the currents
of rising seas and whirl
through the wordworld,
the ones who begat them forgotten
as they rap, whatsapp about
the gulf stream's off-switch, act up in
the streets sans mouth mask/Mund Maske/
kǒuzhào/máscara/māsaka;
as, distanced/calm/frantic
in bedsits/apartments/flats,
they like/link to/follow
what matters, click
for a better planet.

What's that, coming
out of those high-rises—
that chorus/clap/joint shout
in present simple unison?
Tīng/écoute/listen.

THE ISLE OF WIGHT

Under the swollen, bloated sun, seagulls
take flight—they've got this knack
of escape at the flap of a wing. Guiltless
I eat my picnic, do a Sudoku but feel guilty
spending my summer in Ventnor again.
Only birds have free movement off islands,
the right to roam across the seas. Those bodies
beached on Lesbos lack such prowess –
stuck on the sands, wingless., their plight
three lines in The Wight County Press
while here's me in my bright new beachwear
down on the crowded sands at Shanklin,
swimming, picking shells from rock-pools,
breeze drying my feet as I lie; while over there
are border guards, look-out posts, barbed wire,
me using the paper to shield my eyes, hold
the swollen sun at bay; while along the front
there's bloated British bodies everywhere –
this holiday island just like theirs over there –
the days flying, seagulls flying between us.

PORTRAIT BY THE ARTIST'S WIFE

I start with several triangle noses
round his face's oblong. On his chin
a startled eye, one of four. Skin: blue.
All down his jumper's stripes, lips
puffing on pipes. Or puckered at women.
Dora, for one. His beret a disk
up on edge. I roll it into his visage
like a circular saw, slice off an isosceles.
Crimson spatters his sketches—
of her, of all the others. My silly dope—
I loved you more than them! Our Max
and Ernest grown into fine young men;
daughter Nora adoring you
like her mother before her.
Backdrop? Why, a spuming mountain—
genius fountaining!

I WOULD FAINT LIKE IN THE MOVIES

but when I did, they'd ignore me,
my unconsciousness boring—
not the fall of a baddy they'd shot
or garroted or karate-chopped.
The boys played on: I was
one man less to chase.

but I'd still faint, and wait and wait
for a gallant rescuer to act shocked
at first, then take me in hand, and wanly
I'd thank him for slaking my thirst,
his flask of mead tendered with a surprised
realization of love to my rosebud lips—

again and again I'd rise from the playground
and re-try that scene. If only they'd
pick me up, one on each limb—
four warriors carry their dying queen.

KINDNESS VISITS MEI MEI'S CAFÉ

I watch a film call 'Black coal thin ice'. This film less talking, more images impressive. Oh dear, the black coal goes into my heart. Feeling like piece of coal on conveyor belt among many pieces of coal. What is my destination? To be burned, only.

Life is such busy but make me sad. Only a slave in the café, seven days the same, very disappointment. In the morning wake up, brain is empty or cried because dreams disappear—classmates laugh in dormitory, future bright... Were we happier when poorer?

Yesterday two men from foreign came the café when my mood was dark. I took order, prepared some dishes in kitchen with husband then offered the dishes to the men. One dish not correct. Maybe I mistake, I did one more dish they did not ask.

The men discuss with each other. One of them said no problem, we eat it. I see his think: *it is at night, a lot of restaurants closed for food, so late, we should be happy they still make.* He smile and stop his friend to correcting my mistake.

> This man help me in my heart,
> make brave. For kindness is rare.
> I hear the dispute everywhere,
> see fighting. But when kindness,
> life is fair, not walk on thin ice.
> Not slave. Not spite. Not burned, only.
> Classmates phone me. Husband nice.
> In darken world, kindness is light.

BITCHY DRESS

Soon as we're curtained in the cubicle
she bitches about my body, ruches
on my hips, catches my skin in her zip,
snickers out of her buttonholes
you'll never do me up, sneers nastily
at my balcony bra, my silicon plums—
your breasts don't fit my darts.
Your built wrong. Strapping.
Don't expect to have doors opened
looking like that. What's on your head?
Do they make stilettos in size eleven?
Are those man-hands manicured?
Where's your string vest? –

and she goes on trying to resist
but I edge my body in, bit by bit.
Submit, bitch. This is me.

THE THING SAID

The Said Thing is said as a statement of fact—
that climate change, Gaza and social breakdown
mean the end is nigh—when, late afternoon, I drop by
for my annual shock, entering family like a plunge-pool
of siblings, babies and newly-teenaged,
of mournful elders mottle-ankled in armchairs,
my aunty still fascist though senile, Jan Prozac'd out,
Mum in the usual head-dress (antlers), a skeletal niece
with a nauseous eye on her nan's festive buffet

and the man-talk about Keir Starmer and footie till
my two-pen'orth on the apocalypse and how glad I am
I haven't brought kids into all this—how words can sizzle
like firecrackers, be the final straw for a milk-breasted sleep-
deprived hyper-sensitive in-law who massively over-reacts

but there's bombs falling as we speak, there's ice
melting, the homeless having their tents confiscated
and you're doing Happy Families, I yell, there's a world
beyond this sitting-room, these mince pies, smelly nappies,
turkey rolls, paper hats, tinsel, telly—as all eyes turn to
the King, and I say I'm certainly not listening to him either,
I'll see you next year, and we all say Merry Christmas!

MISADVENTURE

The sled's runners sliced into
Antarctica's taut satin ice-sheet.

A loud crack. Schlupfs shot onto
our goggles but we didn't turn back.

A light flakefall started, pixellating
the nunataks, the lines behind us lost.

Ahead cyberhaze, sledging alongside us
in toggled snowsuits our childhoods.

We crossed the lost track's last rutch without
knowing it, the huskies pulling us over the shrit.

It was me who shot the looming shape, laughing
hearing my toy cap-gun again, pop pop pop

but at that the dogs leapt across the crack
bolted off into the sun's white eye, left us

with only a sled and a dead bear to battle the climate,
trapped on an unmapped, melting islet.

MUCHLY

for tucking me up on your couch
with hot toddy and ibuprofen
when i land on you frozen

having walked in the rain
having no bus fare
having only the clothes im stood up in

for moaning i dont dress right
jeans that sop up water
bare midriff

whatever they hand out
at the centre
or what i can find in the bins

thanx, but thing is, i want to feel
our climate. im wearing this flimsy jacket
because it lets it in

YOUR ATTENTION PLEASE
After Peter Porter's nuclear attack poem, 1983

meet on the canal path
twelve noon
no cause for alarm

(instructs the town mayor
a short man
from the top step
of the cenotaph
through the megaphone)

a mutation has hit Bradford
the order is head south-east fast
avoiding Doncaster
walk in convoy
there'll be boats to Ostend
bring sandwiches
pack other food that will last
essential medicine
one toy per child
family photographs
no wheeled luggage
strictly rucksacks
these rules must be stuck to
check twitter for updates
wear weatherproofs
and strong boots
snow is predicted
important note
this convoy is restricted to
passport-holders

MY AXEMAN EX

He'd call out *bye love*, automatic,
my leather-jacket love-deaf lumberjack,
dropping the latch as he left with
rucksack, chainsaw, toolbox and axe.

If he now came back, his actual knock
on this locked door would axe into
my clear-felled wasteland, hack
at this last stump I'm clung to.

TRAVELODGE, 25TH DECEMBER

long, narrow single bed
a black rectangle, sideways.
big bland rectangular wall.
empty wardrobe a vertical rectangle.

rectangular window onto a
car-park marked out in rectangles
and a rectangular shed. the moon
a hard white nail-clipping.

gloom. table rectangular, mirror a rectangle
reflecting rectangular shed and hard white moon.
door beside black-sideways-rectangle of
single bed also a rectangle.

on the rectangular bedside table, the remote—
a particularly narrow rectangle.
the 'on' button rectangular.
thumb an oblong.

THE IKEA CAFÉ, SHANGHAI

Winter scene: brightly floodlit building site
a socket between long, strong verticals –
all the new high-rises barricading out light,
a brick-built apartment block, red banners
billowing down it—*zhong guo,* something *ren, xiao,*
toy-townish forecourt, little privets in pots

as night falls; as oblong windows pop awake,
constellate; as the white lights of trucks whip along the
speedway-on-stilts that spans the horizon where steel
is strung taut between pylons way up from the streets'
crazy looping messes of wires—un-disentangleable
black lacework crudded with demolition dust

till deep darkness falls at last over the land
and the geometry of tower blocks fades,
turns toy-sized, twinkly, and here I am.
Perhaps this whole thing's been a stupid plan,
this workaday Tuesday sipping coffee, tapping along
to a pop song, church bells and robins a world away

this Christmas Day in Ikea, Pudong,
tissue stars twirling over the tills.

DONKEY

The donkey in the story had no proper tack.
Mary in a hijab-thing was balancing
bareback, no reins, nothing
as he plodded through dunes on a page
that had stars done with glitter-glue.

In my world, donkeys lived at the seaside.
I had a go on one. Its body-hair rasped
my sandy thighs and it smelled of holiday.
Yes, there were dunes, but this was real,
not a fairytale like in the Children's Bible.
I knew by then there was no Santa.
Animal heat came up at me, donkey poo
landed splat on my brother's foot
and I could feel a heart beating.

ACKNOWLEDGEMENTS

Some of these poems have appeared in T*he Honest Ulsterman, Shearsman, The Blue Nib, The Last Stanza, The Doubleback Review, Feed, The Grande Dame Literary Review,* and *America Magazine* (Jesuit Review of Faith and Culture).

www.ingramcontent.com/pod-product-compliance
Lightning Source LLC
LaVergne TN
LVHW041327080426
835513LV00008B/616